A Window
Through to Your
SOUL

🖤 ZOË HICKERSON 🖤

Contents

Queen of hearts

I can barely look after myself
Now look what's landed on the proverbial shelf
Unsatisfying
Soul destroying
Little snide remarks
I will run to the park to stop my fuming
It's overwhelming
Self criticising
Saying that piece of puzzle doesn't quite fit
I want to spit and spit
Until fire rages through
Expressing myself like this is it good for you?
Tears smart my eyes
Who should eat humble pie?
This is bemusing
It's almost amusing
What's on the political agendas?
Where no one knows their right from their left
Sometimes I'm like the Brexit clause
It's just the start where it's deftly paused
Like the ubiquitous Queen of Hearts
The opposite direction looks appealing
I want to do some healing
I can barely look after myself
It's a well known book off the shelf
Look I'm not stupid
I'm not looking for Cupid
Rushing me won't get it done
I'm like I've been in a domestic

The aftermath is hectic
Time has been a slow healer
I know we glorify death
We look upon those as weak
We battle day by day to make it through the week
Months creep by with a cheer
My goodness you are still here
Obviously I've made the right choice
It gets harder and harder with that niggly voice
To think that I have
To think that I haven't
It's the small things that set you off
I don't want someone to shake me wondering if I did it on purpose
Who wants to join that circus
When there are signs that smack you right in the face
That says a warm welcome to the human race

Roaring

I'm getting anxious with your constant
Yelling and swearing
I know you're delusional
Fuck mate it's getting rather boring
To hear your constant roaring
I used to be quite thick skinned
Now it's only skin deep
I'm feeling emotional with your ranting and raving
I know it's not personal
I don't know what you are craving
And I know it not Tourettes
Give us a break
From your constant roaring
We will see you in the morning

Waiting

What are you waiting for
Waiting makes my skin crawl
What am I waiting for
Waiting here there everywhere
The anticipation setting alarm bells off in my brain
Making me feel sick in my stomach
Making it tie in knots
Feeling stranded is no one else like me
I get this feeling I want things to hurry up
Waiting for time to slow
Waiting for time to quicken up
It makes me nervous I should be there by now
I'm sorry I'm one of those annoying people
It's set in my brain it's set in my DNA
An automatic response to where I have to be
Breaking out in beads of sweat if there is any kind of delay
Have to stop thinking
Try to make myself late
Others do it with consummate ease
Still waiting to try
Life is full of waiting
Life is full of wasted moments
Waiting to push the daisies up
I'm in my own time frame
It's just me not wanting to be left behind
Waiting for nothing is something I can't do
If we wait for nothing what are we going to do
Waiting or staying what's best for you

Hanging around

How did I fill my time
Just sitting around
Staring blankly at the tv
No purpose no nothing using all my energy
How did 1 thing take all day
Thinking I was busy
Just hanging
The brain stops to reboot it's self
You start to think and look back upon yourself
Was I really that unmotivated
Why didn't I see
I can't believe I was that blind
Time waits for no man or woman
Now that I can
I'm doing things now that stretches my mind
Every so often a memory of the far past pops up
The shackles shaken off
Wow I enjoyed doing that
I haven't done it in a while
Why do we stop and stare
When there are things out there
Growing as a person differently
Hanging around purposely
Time passes you buy when you're blindly hanging around

In my shed

Sitting here contemplating
Why we have been put here
To be given a second or third chance
What do I want
I want no capitulating
To learn by my mistakes
To have an awesome shed
Did I really want to end up dead
In my sound proof shed
I'd have everything laid out
Just in case I want to shout it out
I could make a mess with DIY
I could spread
I could saw
I could sew
I could also spread some noise
Only for the next door neighbour
To complain about the dum dum crash
FYI it's me drumming it in
Oh it's you OMFG
I hope you play another tune
I only arrived in June
It would be warm
It would be my safe heaven
Nobody else just me
Contemplating life ahead
Everything positive
No more mumbling and grumbling
I don't want to be dragged down to those depths
I've already climbed a thousand steps
What do I do now
Somehow

A message will get filtered through this is
your passage go straight ahead
In your cosy safe shed
I don't want to lose
I want to be set loose
From the drudgery
Am I being greedy to want more out of life
Life was put on hold
For so many days
I have time to make up for they were not wasted
I learnt a lot about myself learnt that I'm not as resilient as before
It takes time and energy to fight everyone's battles
Pick and choose which one you want to win
As the quieter ones are always within
Their shed of their dreams

Concrete shoulders

I was encased in my own concrete hell
I would take everything on face value
Just black and grey
No colour between my head
I'd shut my eyes this dark concrete shutter would close
me in, weighing my concrete shoulders down.
Such a weight on your back
My mood was always flat
Everyday another brick
Until it reached the bottom of my neck
Shuffling around
Shoulders down
Until I was my own brick wall
Showing no colour at all
Ideas and life would bounce around my wall
Weeds would grow and spread
Choking me slowly
So opaque
No osmosis for me
I have no idea how to break it down
No tools, no voice
One day the sun came out
Warming the concrete dark
Gradually spreading warmth to the weeds
turning into tiny white daisies
Worming their way through the cracks
spreading and creeping north
I wake with a daisy poking me in the eye
Bees humming around spreading their pollen
I sneeze I cough I spread a tear
Concrete shoulders shaking with fear of what be holds
I have more light

A little angel has arrived
To sit and listen
She stays night and day twinkling away
She makes me feel comfortable
Today I have to go for it is time to shake yourself free.
Oh no little one please come back I don't have
the wherefore all to sustain the fall
Tears rolling down my wall I am shaken free partially
My concrete shoulders leaving dust of the reminder
when I was destined for anonymity

Peculiar author

It's uncomfortable
People knowing my inner thoughts
When I was at my most vulnerable
It sends shivers everywhere
It makes me think
That I'm not the most literate of people
Whilst I pieced myself back together
They sound immature
That's what I'm thinking for sure
Why are people so interested
Whether I made it alive or dead
They are personal to me
It's really peculiar
To be on the other side
How can I see it will help others to flip to the bright side
That there is light at the end of every peculiar funnel,
We struggle every day for that light of hope
Sometimes you need a periscope
I'm in my own submarine encapsulated in the water below
Pressure from every side it's progress is slow
Looking up to see if things will get in the way
What are my words going to convey
Oh yes that was me then
Oh boy I felt it when
It really is peculiar
I'm doing it for myself
Not to have every book on the shelf
It's not what I'm about
I'm helping me
We shall see how it goes
If I'm helping others that's ok I suppose
whether I want to write any more prose

I should be proud of what I've done
I'm more excited about the spine
Because that's where we're strong
It's really most peculiar
An author going forth spreading the news of
how we defuse when we are in the dark

The new one

My concrete jungle has enslaved me with my thoughts
Troubling me with what's to come
Maybe undoing the good I've done
Feeling nervous behind these walls
I can see etched are some of my darkest thoughts
No one can help
No one can see
It is up to me to make her see that I'm
not the fool she once believed
Someone help me
Someone vouch for me
For I see trouble ahead
My concrete jungle has me captured
I feel I'm in flight mode
Does she look at all our work
Does she stop and stare and see the frightened little bird captured
and enslaved by these concrete walls of darkest thoughts
A thousand years ago these walls were bombed
With sands of time they have etched the pain that
came their way, that had come my way
A sand storm so strong no one believed it true
Where in the middle you see me thrashing around trying to gather
these thoughts, tiny bits of sand turn into my concrete wall
My anxiety enslaving me again
I'm a prisoner in my own concrete jungle
I have had the diamond key to let me out

Zoë Hickerson

Each time it has slithered from my grasp, a haughty
laugh from those enslaved who rejoice in captivity
I'm based in reality
I want to break free from the concrete jungle of no personality
Help me now
Help me please
Give me the diamond key I beg you please

Things change

Things change in your mind
Through the end of the tunnel
An onward and upward struggle
To fight the terrorism in your head
Putting your own barriers in the way, that knocks you to the floor
Things do change
I'm going to stay to fight it out, until I knock it out the park.
Though self doubt gets in the way
Going round and round, until you're tangled in scratchy
weeds, leaving their itchy signature. Reminding you have been
comfortable in the entrapment of your negatively geared life.
Back and forth, light and dark with your curdled thoughts.
Things will change
You won't realise until you stand and ponder
the proof of self development
Wiping your hands free of the dirt
Staying put believing in yourself is the key
Stand tall
Feel relaxed
Laugh out loud
I know I've developed
I know I've got skills
I know things change
I know I've changed
What I don't know is what it looks like

Pondering Life

We all know life carries on regardless
We all know life does end
You don't think it will happen
Until you see the signs
A once vibrant person
The life and soul
The shadow of their former self
You know that this will be the last
I can't see it yet
I felt it in the phone call
I can ponder and realise that life has an end date
You don't want it happen
You have to be ready to travel
It will leave a massive hole
I believe in the spiritual
That makes it easier
Not for everyone involved
The passing of time
The passing of the hour
Until their final breath
I'm so glad my words touched you
I don't know what things will make it better
I don't know what we will do
I know life will carry on
With a gap in the earth not wide enough to fill
I hope people realise as they travel
That you have moved mountains

Cuckoo

Thank you for believing in me
I don't know why
Believing in recovery
It's a long voyage of self discovery
Sometimes I get a wriggle on
Sometimes I don't
It depends on the day
It depends on the dollar
I never know myself
When dark thoughts hit me on the shelf
Sometimes my anxiety is out in force
Wondering if I stay the course
I believe in myself some of the time
Wondering how I got there time after time
Things work like clockwork
Somethings are a bit cuckoo
I guess that one life's peculiarities
How your brain is wired
Armed full throttle with strategies to go from A to B
Sometimes without any difficulty
I go straight to Z every now and then
Finding the strength to get myself back again
Swimming through toxic waste of strangest thoughts
Picking what's right and what's wrong I'm that sort
Sometimes I just look up and everything is clear again
Wondering what all the confusion was about
I guess I'm meant to be here without a doubt

Get off your arse

My body aches
My mind is numb
I've got a burst ear drum
My get and go has got up and left
Everything is taxing
Everything is complicated
Spending excess energy on mindless tasks
Sitting around is time consuming
Am I going to get better is what I'm assuming
It's an upward battle
My body is knackered
I don't want to be sent to the knacker's yard
My brain still functions
It goes into gear
1st gear and reverse is all I can muster
I'm getting cross because I'm so lacklustre
What's the next step I have no clue
What I want is the next conundrum
What do I wish to see
What do I wish to conquer
Why and wherefores
Stop asking questions
Get up do
This is how you will discover the renewed you
Get off your arse it's getting wider
Get up and go through the ranch slider

I know

I'm feeling lost in this world
I know what I have to do
I've come out of the darkness into the light
I want my creativity to flourish
I'm feeling sad
I'm feeling blue
I know what I have to do
The more I hate this place
The more depressed I feel
The more I think
The more I want to quit my job
I need the money
I need the stability
I want a challenge
Is it really what I need to do
Do I know what I want
A new challenge of courses and creativity
I'm going to enhance my knowledge
Use it to my advantage
It's exciting
It's boldly going where I've not been before
Let's hope I'm here for more
Not in a stagnant pile of nothingness
Not in the black
I need to listen

I need not to be distracted
Tingling in my fingers
Warmth in my toes
Wondering where this is going to go
I really don't want to be in my job anymore
I'm sensitive to negative
Sensitive to the environment
After a power nap I feel more positive

How do I see

How do I see myself now?
A year ago I was having thoughts of ending it
Crossing off ways that I thought would be too easy
Then finding it knowing it was scary
I can easily think I'm on the brink
Finding those thoughts are easier now
I don't feel intimidated
How could I, how could you
Dark thoughts are easy to entertain
Just fuel your fire until the very end
I don't want to keep going round and round
Ending up where I began
How do I see myself now?
I'm not stuck
My mind in constant turmoil
Good days
Bad days
Days in the middle where I could go either way
Having had to proof read the lot, being an
author set my thoughts tumbling free
What I didn't think was it
Has set my brain on fire
My mind is full of a toxic waste dump
Where I could easily go thump
My head is sick of storing all these memories
The door that slams open to the next
Silently closing on the one before
As they mumble and jumble together
How would you see me now?
Do I look a lot less lost?

Zoë Hickerson

You presume I'm happier
I'm finding it easier to deny it
How do I see myself now?
That is a difficult question to ask
It's a love hate relattionship the place where I work
I'm finding it hard to realise
It's a sad place
It's difficult to save face
I work with a different pace
It's awful to feel this way
I don't know, I just don't know
Words can't describe it
Don't give a bullshit reason
I just don't understand

Broken dreams

Yellow eyes fixated on me in the dark
Watching every breath
Listening to every snore
Prowling around the bed
Gracefully avoiding the iPhone charger
Yellow eyes wandering around the room
He's on the prowl
He can smell nightmares
He jumps without a murmur
His wet nose resting on mine
As I exhale a breath he's sitting proudly
upon my chest, whiskers twitching
Waiting to inhale my final breath
Not tonight
I'm not ready for you to it take so soon
Pawing at the covers looking at me in a state of undress
Wanting to take my breath under duress
Inhaling nightmares gives yellow eyes his power
A tiny tear releases, bringing alarm as I
stir and move around the bed
With lightening reactions he leaps off my chest
Unable to concentrate with tonight's test
He bounds up and out into the wilderness
Leaving a claw mark as a reminder of tonight's broken dream
I awake myself with a silent scream
My chest feels heavy
My mouth feels dry
I sense that something has gone awry

Doing it for ourselves

Another surprising moment
As I realised I haven't been doing
Doing what we did on our days off before
Another pinging moment
Hard cold evidence that I haven't been around
Why I don't I understand is why we go way behind there
It's enjoyable these life little treasures
It's a sit up sniff the roses once again
That we have so far to go
After we let ourselves go
It's sad when you think your other half
has been carrying you through
Through the pyre
Through the journey along into the other side
Not knowing if you're going to be the same inside
Aware that you will be thinking differently
'You're going to leave me
I don't know when'
How do we remain positive that our relationship is going to thrive
We are going to strive
To make it to the other side
I've never been in this situation
It's seems selfish that I have been working
on myself all the way through
Not noticing how it affected you
Waiting for the real me to turn up
Slip up after slip up

You waited for me to emerge
We work on ourselves together to reignite our special days
Picking up the pieces of my once disorganised life
I hadn't realised I didn't see
I must been blinded by dark negativity

Zoë Hickerson

Will you still love me

Every time I say no
Are you having a laugh or are you being serious
Every time I've been horrid I've notched it in my heart
Knowing I'm doing it makes it harder for me
As I see it slices you in half
I remembered the time I had a drink and
was a petulant little shrimp
You still came to see me in Hookers corner,
even though I didn't need a pimp
I woke myself up that day knowing it does us harm
You think I forget these things
Or we blame it on Donk
That pesky little soft toy sitting on the chair
Donk & Ditto make a right old pair
We're growing old together
I'm still young at heart
You've gone grey and I'm going white
I'm still quite impulsive and need to be reigned in
Hey that's me feet first and then dangle in
I have changed
I'm still short
The changes are for the best
Skills that we need to sort out Donk and his crew
I apologise when I get ratty
I apologise when I'm short
You can see when the lights are on and no one's home
We all need guidance
We all need a hand
Let's not dig our heads in the sand

Change is good
Change is challenging for it makes us sit up and
think of who we are now and not then
Do you still love me
Even when I say no

Zoë Hickerson

Sorcerer's Apprentice

I'm the Sorcerer's Apprentice
There's a lot I can't fix
I can't do any magic tricks
I feel so disempowered it's tragic
I think I was hired for my logic
An angel twinkling around making sure I do no harm
I've got a sense of dread that fills this room
I don't know it just happens
My thoughts are pretty toxic
I know I'm not stuck
I must have dipped my head in the toxic waste truck
Lots of memories some good mostly bad
Are making me sad
I don't know how
I'm minding my own business, in comes this plough
Raking up thoughts and feelings that I don't really want right now
I've failed the first lesson and probably others too.
I've learnt from them
This is what gives it value
I'm trying to wave my magic wand
It just spits and splutters with acrid smoke
Why In fairy tales everything comes smelling of roses and bespoke
I'm not going to admit defeat
Even if I have to keep trying and trying
I don't want to be a failure
I will just be another statistic
I'm not made of plastic you know
I know I can grow from this you keep telling me so

So why is it so dam hard
Getting the mixture right,
Lotions and potions
A sprinkle here, a bit of sprinkle there
I know I can't do magic
I'm just the apprentice letting life go drifting on
Letting other people go casually by
It's something that makes me cry
I've lost my hold on the world
I thought I had it figured
All I have is a wand that's wrongly triggered

Things that I want

I'm feeling upset
The tears are flowing
I hadn't cried for so long I didn't know which way I was going
Things that I want
And things that I can't have
Make me feel immature in a woman's body
Teenage feelings of love and wanting
Adult feelings of lust and lost hope
I suppose they are all human emotions
Particularly strong at the moment
I don't understand I should be happy
Instead I look and turn around
Unsure of what I see
Unsure of what
I guess I miss everyone around me
I guess I miss my chaotic family
I can't turn back time
I don't think I want to, as I'd be stuck somewhere else
Probably not thinking of what I'm thinking right now
Threats to harm
Threats to disappear
If I did that I'd only reappear in someone else's
body hijacked along the heavenly highway
Karma has a funny sense of humour
Getting you back when you least expect
Who on earth would be its prime suspect
Crying for now has quietened these feelings
I was trying to dampen them down with different dealings

All it would do was make me frown
I tried the train to bid au revoir
All it did was break my reservoir
Now I have stopped
These feelings have dissipated
I know we're never going to be acquainted
It only ever really hurts me
To live with it I feel partially emotionally equipped
Crying helps with the ginormous dips

Granddads old vest

I didn't go to the gym for 8 months
No wonder I got this great lump
Working on yourself mentally
Goes with working on yourself physically
You can't see what it's doing
You can feel every sore
It's strange now I'm going back I don't feel as poor
Where did my motivation go
Where had my inner voice gone
It was trying to work out what was wrong
So insular in yourself
You feel so selfish
Oh my goodness what had I become
I knew it was at least six months
You have that intuition
Mumbling to whoever is back there should
I or should I not go battling on
Going back battling that inner demon that
was rattling round my head
Let's rattle them bones and see if you're still around my nut
Grumbling little demon is there alright
I'm going to squash him against the weights
I'm going to ride him into the virtual sunset
Up hills and down valleys I puff as I get fitter
Hoping that going back has made me richer
I managed to sweat and my face is a little red
It hasn't been too bad

Placing yourself on top that every day you give is your best
So many layers of self-discovery
You have to realise there will be highs
There will be times when you feel like putting
on your granddads old holey vest

Back to the beginning

Yellow pus
Escaping from every pore
I've climbed and I've climbed to reach the point of no return
What have I been given to reach this pinnacle
I've scrapped and I've scraped my knees and elbows are red roar
I haven't been taking care of myself as they are all very sore
Pustules of yellow stuff creeping out
If I squeeze a fountain of murky pus shoots across the floor
Laying here wondering what got me here before
I thought I was on top blimey that was a little immature
So I stopped working on myself
Thinking I had made it free at last from the misery
Boy I was wrong
Boy I was premature
Starting again I have to be twice as strong
I'm 3 steps behind from where I was before
This time the rocks are biting into my skin, it's
like pouring alcohol into an open sore
The more I keep trying the bigger they become
Oh boy I was stupid
Taking things for granted
For I smell quite putrid
The moral of this is you can't stop working or believing in yourself
Whether it be a tear jerker
Or a monster blockbuster
You have the script to your own life storey

General election

We hang on precariously
Hanging on by the quick of our nails
You're a bit buggered if you chew your nails
Hanging onto hope in life that you won't get tired
Too tired to hang in
Too tired to have belief
Everyone you know is behind you
Giving you gentle nudges along
Some a great big shove to get you over the
edge to show the light is ahead
Your mood is set for the day when you get out of bed
Don't give me false hope
For it is a competition out there
My anxiety is holding
I just don't want a negative thought that will send me back to bed
I'm up for the day
A little slower than before
I'm ready to get myself going
Bloody hell the Welsh language is strange
A good laugh to brighten your day
I'm delaying the truth by evading my feelings in my head
I'm giving myself hope
That my policies are worth voting for
For I am my own general election
I'm hoping positivity will get the majority
A swing to the bright side
I am unsure what is predicted
To get my self realected
I'm hoping I haven't cast my vote too soon
I hold my breath as it may be too early to predict
I watch with bated breath for I may have misjudged myself

Where has my ummph gone

Some days are a bit flat and
I have silence in my head
a hurtful silence I don't have things running through my head
Anxiety is there and it's under control
I don't know which I prefer fighting the thoughts,
working on myself or feeling blah
I don't really want my thoughts rushing in all at once
I don't feel I've got the humph
I have to drag myself around
It's really strange
I think I'm deranged
With the silence my head
I want to clean my ears
I think they're blocked
No it's just the silence in my head
My head feels heavy
My head feels empty
I just sit and ponder
Lose track of time
I've been sitting here all the time
My Grrrrrr has got up and left
Bring it back someone please
I have motivation
I have been organised
Maybe it was an organised crime that stole the thoughts in my head
The silence in my head
I'm sending a wanted poster
A picture of my head what does it look like
Wanted a head that is alive
With the fight to drive

It makes me feel tearful
The energy has gone
It's not a good feeling
The organised crime in my head must've done some dirty dealing
I'm not sure how it's come about
I'm going round and round about trying to find the cause
I guess someone's pressed paused
Someone press the play button please to release
this flat bottomed piece of nothingness
Do I feel worthless
Do I feel a burden
Pretty good questions to ask yourself
Today is hard it's like a grey cloud has
desened I can feel the pressure
It's going to defend its self from the black that's looming
There's a lot more going on than I think
I've got to get myself out of this pretty quick
A piece of Kit Kat has me triggered
I think that was it I've finally figured

Rate your mood

Making you think outside the box
Rating you mood
10:10
Don't be silly
You're having a laugh
No one's ever going to be that happy
Oh ok
Shall I go lower
What do you want
You want me to learn numerousy
I'm really a silent assassin
1:10- 10:10 what does it really mean
It's just numbers that you can see
Look you've done your work
Talking to people
You can bluff your way through
Or you can sit and stare
What do you mean
It's crazy it's stupid
Why can't you say how you feel
Just say I feel like shit
Instead of having numbers on a stick
Who came up with it anyway
You can see people's awkwardness they want to fly away
You can see their minds ticking over
Did I really mean to say that number
People dwell on the last thing you said
Or run with it instead
I'm feeling blue

What does that number mean for you
I'm feeling crazy everything is hazy
So what does it mean when I can't give you a number
You look a bit confused
I'm quite bemused
With all these numbers rattling in my head
You really need to go back to university
To get a maths degree these numbers never really quite compute
There isn't a quote
You get on my goat
Some say 1 being the worst
Or one being the best
No wonder I'm in here I just wanted to get things off my chest
You're an annoying little pest
Do you see the numbers on my forehead
like they've been branded in
You really need to have a handle in
As you can see I've taken pity
Here she comes with the numbers
Let me go hide or shall I refuse
Should I act confused
I'd really like a decent slumber
You're making yourself even dumber
Here I go counting sheep
Bloody hell these numbers make me weep
Just give me some medication
I can see your dedication
You've worn me down
My hands are up
Have it your way
Here Is how I rate my mood at 4:10

Zoë Hickerson

My impulsive whim

I've done it again
Not thought of my behaviour
Not thought of the consequences
Hurting the ones closest to you
Yeah it hurts inside
Well that's justified
As a selfish feeling
That's left her reeling
Maybe not thought of the bigger picture
Maybe I did
Why are you so concerned about people's reactions
Maybe it's a distraction
Of what's going to happen
Knowing about how family tears you up inside
I can see it does
I don't know how to console you
I'm feel like I'm a spectator looking from the other side
Don't keep barraging me with your thoughts of how it's going to be
I start to creep inwardly
Shutting down
It brings the fears of leaving
I know I've done it, I know it hurts
I can't give a reasonable reason
We have to live with the consequences
Of my impulsive behaviour
Where do we go from here
Tread carefully my dear
Don't blame it all on yourself
That's not how it works
You have to give me some so I can learn myself

Radical acceptance

Radical acceptance
Sitting freely and let your thoughts come in
Feeling the hurt
In your mind and body
Accepting the pain it's caused
What I don't understand
I know the pain I've felt it
I've thought I had forgiven myself
Letting go of the guilt
Practising the train
Why do I want to feel it again
I'm happy working on myself
Maybe this is another level
That puts you on the straight and narrow
Sometimes I shoot myself with my own poisonous arrow
Maybe it's my complacency
Let's try another agency
To try and figure it out in someone else's place
You get unwanted guests renting your body space
They leave leaving a huge trace of destruction
Where you're unable to function
It's venting on another level
It works for some
Accepting what you've done
Accepting what's happened
Using creative tools
Work in reflective writing
Why should I keep on biting

Zoë Hickerson

Maybe I need a walk through of the event
Where will I be after radically accepting that
my thoughts were a bit screwed
Where I miscued
Changed my life for the better
Where I gained more empathy
I certainly don't want sympathy
Radically accepting I've changed for the good
Accepting it's all good in my hood
How's that for complacency

Answer yourself

My least favourite question I ask myself
Have I left myself behind
You want my true answer
Or do you want to bluff my way through
so I don't hurt my own feelings
Honestly yes
It depends on the hour
To turn everything sour
Yes I have left myself behind
Sometimes it looks like I don't care
You don't know what's going on beneath there
I'm trying to keep my inner resolve
My opinion doesn't always count
It's not always right as we get down upon ourselves
I don't really know where I'm going
I never know how the day will progress
I do care I just need my inner tigress
I think I can handle the pressure
Then something comes along
I've just got to get over myself
To stop thinking negatively
And start thinking differently
Questioning like prime minister's question time
I will stand upon the gravel
To let my opinion travel
Question me how you want
Because I've already visited the swamp
Do I hold my self responsible

To let someone go at their darkest hour of need
Somehow somewhere this thought has floated
past and planted another seed
I've never thought of it before
It makes you think that
I've never thought at all
I think I've nailed it on the head
My mind is blank
My hair is dank
My thoughts aren't in the black
They're just circling somewhere else
It's just me trying to find where I fit
All this battling has made me stand tall
Run like a dog after its favourite toy
It's tongue lolloping from side to side
No suicide note
For you to fuss over me like a nanny goat
I've no idea what to seek
What to grasp
Or to hold onto
Who to turn to in my darkest hour of need
I will turn to baking
And knead my dark thoughts away

Responsibility

Where does your responsibility lie
Why does it have such a cutting feel
Is it another process of my grieving
Is it part of forgivness
Why does it hurt so bad
Why has it taken so long
Does it lie in wait for when you're strong enough
crashing into your thoughts like a force 9 gale
Waves of dark green swirling angry sea
Bashing your soul
Destroying your resolve
Abandoning your tenuous grip on life
Wondering if it's going to leave me cold
Have I been stupid enough not to think like this
As it destroys your inner calm
Cutting like a butcher's knife
Straight through the sinew
Straight through the tissue
Leaving strands of old cold congealed blood
Putrefied and leathery
In the killing fields of silent torture
You can't hear the silent screams of anxiety
You can hear the pop of the gun as it goes through their heads
How do I forgive myself of this burden of responsibility
We shall wait and see for the days are long
To see how far this drags on
Am I coming to realise the magnitude
Of how destroying one owns life has affected
me even when it was on their terms

Toot toot

A steam train chugging at speed
A virtual train that travels between our ears
Designed especially not for picking up passengers
Picking up people's thoughts
Delayed now and then by extra baggage
To take on people's clutter
That usually leaves them floundering in the gutter
These trains are specialised
These trains are skilful
They open their doors quietly
And then shut with an almighty crash
Chugging and tooting along
Decluttering the silent torment that lets our brains go free
These trains are never ending
They go night and day 24/7
Use your imagination for the driver is free
There isn't a time table for it can't be predicted
They can't be scripted
Like those negative thoughts that are encrypted into our DNA
They have to be gently teased and squeezed
free, for they are our false beliefs
Arriving quick as a flash
Departing with a whoosh and a sigh
There is no such thing as rush hour
There is no such thing as working to rule, no Trade Unions
No placards with rules and regulations
Always empty on arrival
Bursting at the seams on departure as we
wave our negative thoughts goodbye

Skid marks

Some days I wake up and I smile from within
Not a care in the world
As I drive to work
Other days it's a chore
And why would the world care
If I was feeling anxious
Or tearful
We have to be careful
Of the danger signs
That makes the smoke alarm beep
After not enough sleep
That is the chaos in your head
Too much noise to deal with that
Leaving a skid mark in your conscious
Sometimes too late for the train to come in
Round and round it goes until you're truly deeply emersed
In the fog of unwelcome visitors
Until someone says oi what's going on
I don't know you ask me
I'm just the host with the boy racer skid marks

An unexpected visit from the Dark

You've come to visit me unexpectedly
I was gullible to think I had you conquered
I've answered you again
You're happy for me to stay
You seemed really happy for me to go
In that split second I was strong enough to divert your attention
Through my tears of frustration I was able to maintain control
You held me in your vice like grip
For days others were aware and didn't tell me,
when I looked so tired and distant
Until I had those dark thoughts
It left me reeling that I was so complacent
Thinking I wouldn't have them again
The difference between guilt and responsibility
is a humongous cavern
Responsibility a word that had never been in my thoughts
In my world responsibility cuts like a guillotine
My whole being as a nurse as a person
Responsibility is a particular burden of
obligation, accountable and culpability.
Feeling guilty is sometimes just a throw away comment,
it can be at an end of a sentence with a shrug or a half
smile. Until it rocks your world upside down
I can't say I won't think of this again
Depends on several factors coming together like a perfect storm
I can't guarantee I will come out without thoughts of ending it all

We will work together to sort it out
Using my techniques
Using tenacity
To carry this burden on my shoulders without it damaging my soul
I have to be aware that you sneak up when
my hands are behind my back
Thank you for showing me how strong I am
To answer your poisonous call and to be
able to carry my head held high

Deliverance

I was tested yesterday
I failed miserably
Anxious from the get go
Leaving my lights on
Certainly no one at home
Trying to juggle my time
I was ineffective
Running around like a chicken with its head cut off
Anxious and disorganised
Feeling hot feeling stupid
I was nobody's Cupid
Trying to help a friend
With my wisdom
With my words
I failed with that too
I should've stayed in the loo
Where nobody could find me
Trying to work myself out
No ping or pong moments
Just me wondering what to do
Why does it have to happen
Am I setting a test for me to
Carrying myself around like I've got baggage on my back
Vulnerable from attack from the prisoner cells in my brain
Everything was on lock down
I was in segregation
Freedom to move where I wanted
I was moving in circles round and round I went
Not earning my pennies, not making much
sense, not giving myself time to vent

Airy
Fairy
Not a good look
Why do I let this happen to go on for so long
When I returned everything was a ok
I think I let myself down
My lines get deeper every time I frown
A big line down the middle
Where I give my hair a bit of a twiddle
I'm not really functioning to my capabilities
Just get up and learn instead of wondering about the past
Live for the future for it is now
I will deliver don't you worry
When I'm on form I'm faster than a curry from the night before

Sand

Sand soft as silk running through my fingers, hypnotic as the
crystals fall silently down falling into soft little mounds
Aiding my self expression
No shackles holding me back
No telephone saying it's going to be ok
I know it's going to be okay
As I've peered out of the dark into the light and I like it
Different daily challenges
Challenges I could overcome before
Sometimes finding it difficult to get my way out a paper bag
It would be me in the middle
One with baggage on my back and the other free
Outside will be life going on ahead
Sometimes detailing another path to go down
Until I get back on track
Soft sand breaking my fall
Crunching harmlessly under foot
Mounds of softness without having a care if you got it wrong
It won't criticise it won't blame
Swipe it away and begin again and again
Mould it into different shapes
Or just lay there in the sun
With the sun and breeze caressing your face
Hands sifting gently
Take your worried look of your face, and concentrate
on the coolness through your fingers
The heat of the black sand
Or the softness of the White or, the harsh
stony beeches of your yester years

Take you back to your innocent childhood memories of sand
castles, donkey rides, buckets and spades and Mr Whippy 99's
Or your Grandpa collecting seaweed to predict
the temperature, with a twinkle in his eye
Sea gulls gorging themselves on scampi and chips
Watching in awe as his teeth fall from his lips
Finding shells bleaching them in the sun
Finding sand in your socks and your underpants
Recalling your favourite holiday snaps
Sands of self expression cooling from active play
I wonder what stories they have to say

Plastic fantastic

Where do I rate on the pretending scale
Do we have such a thing
Not sure if its researchable
Do we pretend we're alright
When we're not
Oh dear I drank heavily last night and fell flat on my face
What a disgrace
Was I pretending or was it for real
That my face looks like orange peal
We get rebuked by others
When you really want sympathy and chocolate
Please excuse me from my past, I haven't
really learnt the art of moderation
Are we pretending to pretend the consideration
That our past behaviours are a product of our misspent youth
Or mirrors of our parents
We pretend we are ourselves
In reality were projecting what happened in the past
Where everything went too fast
When they were closeted indoors
Only on two floors
Going blindly
Pretending nothing was wrong
We cheat ourselves out of life lesson
When we search for the pretending button
Get up live for real
Instead of living like a plastic Barbie and Ken
Every now then
We put on that fictitious smile
That stays with you a while

Instead you're gritting your teeth
Cursing with anger with what lies beneath
We put on a brave face
To save us falling from grace
Falling from that perch that seems so far away
Running around the moat
That makes us seem to float
Going round in circles
I'm sick of pretending
It seems never ending
Give out emotionally
It will make sense professionally
Chuck out the plastics they are pretending
Just be careful of overspending
To get your life back into balance

My life flashed before me

My life flashed before me
In that split second I was going to be dead
Hands off the wheel
Heading for the wall
Why am I so calm about it
Why am I not scared
Why did I not have my safety net on
Maybe it was a bluff
Before you do the real stuff
You don't think of others
Only yourself at the point of impact
Would I think oh shit
I've made a mistake
Or would I relax and say do your worst
Because I've worked hard for myself
Now is the time to ease off as you think life is covered
When the black makes another encore
Filling your head with all types of garbage
You have to sift through what's the real truth and what's not
In that split second my brain was going to be mush
Just as well I wasn't in a rush
Slow motion pictures of the air bag exploding forth
As the wall stood firm
The car turning to putty
Who knows what life would be like
Would I be oblivious
Where would my conscious be

Floating through the air or in the road with a
number beside, ready to be photographed
Trying to find a place to settle
Am I in the right fettle
I know it sounds confrontational
Stuff right in your face
You think whoa that's radical

The day that I left

I knew my life was on the right track
Poisonous relationships
The infection spreading across my brow
You had already been infected some how
I could see it creeping along
I wasn't allowed to be myself
It was like the Stepford wives gone wrong
Squeeze me into a bracket
I'd put on my deceitful jacket
That I knew wasn't me
I played along for a while
Until I could deliver the final blow
It's not how I wanted to do it that low
When your resources are depleted
You know of no other way
Strangled in the web of deceit
Enough was enough until it was my way or the long way
The day that I left
I would take an invisible cloak
Remove my things until the bare essentials remain
I've left a lot of places where I had built up stuff I loved
When you're that desperate you have to
leave the things you cherish
Otherwise your soul will perish
My ear was always close to the ground
If you ever came around
Waiting for that tap tap on the door
I'd hit the floor
Go into turtle mode
Slower and slower until you get bored
I would peek out the window and go away with my hoard

The day that I left
I know it was cowardly
I know it was furtive
I knew of no other way
It was my way of escaping
Running to another country is a bit extreme
Here I'm able to live my dream
I've learnt from my mistakes
Learning running away is something I do frequently
I don't do it discreetly
I have to stop
I have to learn
It doesn't stop me thinking about it
The day that I left
I have to stop and listen
To what others are saying if my eyes glisten
For an easy way out
To check myself out
For an easy run
On the run way of escapism, loneliness,
infection, rejection and depletion

Zoë Hickerson

What gives me pleasure

I don't want shoes
I don't want material things
My body aches for the most human of things
What were made for
Relationships
And what we are
Sexual beings
Relationships built on trust and pleasure
Pleasure is what I ache for
That general touch
The softness of our skin
The smoothness of every touch as I caress
I feel your hairs raise as the excitement begins
Tiny beads of sweat
Are the sweetest of things
Knowing your body is as hot as mine
The anticipation of waiting for you to decline
I've waited for so very long
The ache get harder and harder
We have the gentle caress
I'm longing for the rest
Knowing my brain can't go into over drive
It's almost like being driven away it stops so
sharply almost as if it wasn't there
Is it really fair
I can see the flaws
I wouldn't get dirty on the floor
It's been so long
I have to jolly myself along

Furtive looks on certain sites
Even looking longingly at ladies tights
How long does this go on for
You asked me to wait
Without any bait
It's turned the opposite way where we fall apart
I don't think I could make the first move or know where to start
I look with disgust deep down inside
I don't understand why I haven't strayed
Because I don't want you to feel betrayed
It's hard to say it's been years
You don't even tell me why
I know it will cut like a knife deep down inside
I wouldn't know how to sweep what it is aside
We're at a stale mate
Looking at each other's baggage of life's conundrums
How long can this carry on
Before my baggage or my head is finally gone

Im not afraid

I'm thanking you now as I feel strong
My mind abundantly clear
I'm not afraid to show my vulnerability, to you
or another person across the room
It takes strength to hold it in
It shows on the quiver of my voice
I notice and think has anyone else
I start again with clearing my throat
Look up and see intense blue eyes
Listening to every word
A pause
A silence
A silence so loud you can hear a pin drop
An intake of breath from the other side
Wide eyed and shiny
I wait, for I am afraid of the response, is it good or is it bad
Does it show I'm truly mad
Say it again and again
Beautiful words, a shake of their head like time has stood
still, remembering something from their distant past
I know now my writing is from the deepest part of my soul
Where it captures others and tears their hearts
For they would love to express it too
I know not how it came this way
I'm hoping the honesty will stay
I'm aware I show my vulnerability. and the way it shines
through. Down the neural pathways then ink to paper.
Such a powerful thing to capture what you think
I'm not afraid to be in the moment
I'm not afraid to sit and ponder until the magic happens

Don't be afraid to try it once in a while for it is truly liberating
I'm not afraid to carry on with no acceptance
with what I'm trying to convey
That this hurtful soul has been through
so much it's painful to touch
I'm not afraid to say thank you for this opportunity
It may never come again
These maybe short as if to quote
My own suicide note

Zoë Hickerson

Tears

I cry I know not why
I feel vulnerable from attack
From the apathy I see before me
I feel emotional inside as I've spoken freely
I sit and reflect quietly
Everything raw
Things tasting differently from before
A new beginning baring all
It brings everything into focus
That I try not to be selfish
As it has a far reaching impact
People I don't really think about
Maybe I should scream it out
It's funny when I listen it brings a smile to my face the
lady saying on purpose on a mindfulness tape
Not much to smile about now as I feel the tears
Come stinging through
I don't know what I've done
I can't do anything right,
Maybe it is time to give up the fight
Tears clearly flowing
I'm a tad confused
I'm a tad emotional
Just let me be me by myself
I find your presence toxic
I have to leave
For me to be able to breath
New vitality coming forth
Sitting in my car opposite the grave yard

It's not where I want to be digging in the dirt
I just wanted to cry peacefully and feel the hurt
Give me 30 minutes to gather myself
You never know I may get picked up loitering with intent
Don't give into negative thoughts
As they drag you down
How do I cope
That's for me to say and you to find out
My heart is sore
I feel I'm bleeding from every pore
My truthful feelings spilling out in tears
Maybe it numbs the years I thought I was alive
Now I think I've only just begun to survive
A new me emerging from the crystlist that was my prison
Accepting the changes drying my wings of freedom and delicacy
Hoping one day they will be able to break free
and fly away to the brightness of beyond

Zoë Hickerson

A gigantic shift

I feel a deep cavern has been created
I can see the difference in how we interact
You sit
And you sit
On the computer
Or on the phone
I don't understand
I didn't notice when I was internalised
The little idiosyncrasies are bugging me now
I'm afraid of the oil spitting
I'm afraid of this and that
Your especially risk averse it's stifling
I know I have to be careful as my filter is still askew
Give me a chance to shine as I'm not always going to listen
I don't know what I've done today
There's a gigantic shift
It's as wide as the Grand Canyon
You tell me to be sympathetic
I hear you go oooh and ow
I've been with you for quite a while
Is it me today where I need to heal from inside
Or is it because you see the difference
I want to be different
I know it's unnerving
I know there has been a gigantic shift
To see your loved one moving forward
in places you never thought of
I know it's strange for me

I'm enjoying it while it lasts and I want to develop further
I want to go where I have never been before
I'm sorry if you feel this is leaving you behind
I want to make up for what we lost whilst I was in the dark
If I have to do it alone then so be it
It's not what I thought would happen
For fuck sake get up and do something
Where you're not making me feel at a loss

A rant or 2

What was I like until I silently withdrew
Was I that distant
I can't remember the withdrawing
Gradually removing myself
From things I used to enjoy
I'm finding pleasure in things like they are renewed
I used to do so much
Having to give myself that extra punch
Seeing things brighter than before
I've gradually woken up
Like being reborn in your head
I don't feel my age
I feel much younger
For I must be hungry
To stretch myself out there again
I feel my mind is 20
With an old decrepit body
And a sparkling mind that blows people out of the water
Sometimes it feels like a shaken bottle of bubbly
Bubbles going up your nose
Making my eyes water
I feel I've turned many corners and a few 180 degree turns
I hope to have good days
And try to forget the negatives that turn my world around
It used to be the darkest black
Now it's lighter and airy
My advice for anyone
You will come through to the other side
Sometimes longer than anticipated
Times are never stipulated

It depends how hard you try
You will remember to cry
Words that have a deep routed meaning
Will stop you fast, words have many connotations
I stop and look more closely and see how other people hurting
Give them a month or two you will see their personality returning
It really was a blessing
I know more things now than I ever used too
I am able to be empathetic and more enlightened
I maybe more forgiving as I have forgiven myself
I see bits of my personality returning
The yearning to be like others will not disappear
I stand out in the crowd as I have much to be proud

Time after time

Time has a new meaning
Time has a different feel
Time is relaxing now
A calmness between my ears
A calmness in my heart
I can't explain what's happened
Time happens in moments
It seems to have more purpose
It seems to make me smile
I know time waits for no man
It seems time is waiting for me
Maybe it's my time to catch up with how I want to feel
I want to make the most of time whatever I have left
The sand timer trickles through calmly
Calmly powering through is how I feel
I'm obsessed with time
As it seems more peculiar
Time
Time
Tell me why this word matters so much
We shouldn't clock watch during the day
especially at night as we would never sleep
I don't feel bogged down
I feel kinda free
Time has freed me up of the drudgery
Father Time has been precious
Time lengthens the day
Lengthening enjoyment of my day

My new kettle

I'm all in a flumox
With butterflies in my stomach
People have been nice
I've been complemented more than twice
I don't understand
Are they trying to be underhand
To receive such feedback I pull my shoulders back and up
My stomach churns in surprise
Like a fish with a dangly thing in front
Or a donkey with a carrot
I've been handed hope that I can do a good job
It feels very weird
I feel different again
My heart beating my breath catching again
I've spoken freely about my vulnerability
And get shocked answers back
I'm so glad you didn't or you are so wonderful
Don't give me that shit
Your just inflating my over deflated ego
Where it will go down fast
With a pinch or a knock
I can't handle that kind of pressure
It makes my thoughts jumbled
Even tho I should be very humble
Its all in my head
I don't know what to do
It's all very new
It's my inner voice saying your a bag of poo
I know it's going to take a lot of work to work on myself esteem
Just let me get up ahead of steam

Just like a kettle
Filling it up until it whistles or over flows
Where is it now is just around my ankles
I wouldn't mind a halo one that I could manage
Don't let me choke or put it in the garbage
As I'm human after all
Just keep on a steady pace
As we all like watching a fall from grace
It makes me want to cry
All this sickly sweet stuff is too dry
I don't know how to keep myself up
When I think I should shut up
I've never tried to be perfect
I'm learning more about myself
I just need a baseline
Because it's all changed for the good

Huff and a puff

I feel I have a personality
I feel it returning
Those silly things I giggle at
Or the repartee with the Mrs indoors
I have a wide expanse of space
That I have to embrace
It feels cool
It feels enormous
My head feels like it's expanded
You can see the fog through the trees
I'm walking along feeling free
I don't have to count to three
To experience or experiment with life on the up
I'm a bit cagey
As I don't want any false hope
Who knows if it's early day's
There's no text book
You only have to look
At me to know where I am
A little confused with wide ranging stuff
I have to give a big huff and a puff to blow the cobwebs away

Sour milk

Things that you think about
What you least expect to come up
Like regurgitated milk
Sour and it burns on its way up
Leaving a bitter after taste
Things that I think about that get me in a frazzle
Really hurtful things that could knock you around for good
Not things you want to think about when
it's from the Mrs painful past
As you grow as a person and realise what you really want
Thinking you could go further without man's greatest need
I don't know how to talk about it
I've got to be able to set my thoughts free
As it will come tumbling over boiling and bubbling away
burnt sour milk taking ages to wash away
I never thought of running for freedom
Where would I be if my feet did the talking
At the other end of longitude
With the polar blast freezing my heart strings away
What does this tell me about myself
That I care and put others first in pursuit of happiness
Its not something I want to talk about
I have got to bring it out in the open
Burying isn't an option
I wish I can sort it out I my head
Things that you think about before going to bed

I'm scared

I'm scared I will have no more in me
I'm scared this will be it
I'm scared that it will only last this long
I've enjoyed being creative
I've loved the end result
What happens when I've recovered fully
Will there be a space
An emptiness
A hole in my head
Similar to a lobotomy
Without the tell tell scar
I won't have anything to talk about
I wonder what I will do
Will I search for the dark to feel again
Will I enjoy the light
What I've experienced of the light is really really good
I'm scared I will go back down
I'm excited that I can look after myself
I don't like to doubt
Or be quick to assume
That the dark will never reappear
I've returned to the surface
From the murky depths below
Oh boy I feel for others whose recovery is so painfully slow
To see their sadness, to see their emptiness
Was it like this for me during the season
I know I'm in this for a reason
I just need some redirections

Great Aunt Maud

I've had my spiritual awakening
And I've seen the light
The light so energising you don't know what
to do, it opens through any portal
It's quite hard to believe
Unsure of who to tell afraid they will throw away the key
It truly is amazing for an old agnostic to see
I believe there is life in the middle until
they are waiting to be set free
Wandering around trying to find that connection
To tell you it's going to be okay
For you and your spiritual awakening, you don't need
people to tell you, someone is trying to come through
Is it your Great Aunt Maud
Heck no I don't have one of them, you great big fraud
I will connect again when I'm good ready
Ready to release the soul that is floating around on the roundabout
It could've been mine haunting the motorway
Trying to pick the pieces up of me splattered across the road
Giving other's a unique experience who believe in spirituality
Light and darkness so very different and so strangely similar
Both sourced by light at the end of the scale
It takes strength to remove yourself from the dark
It takes more strength to stay in the light
It's easy to stay in the dark as you don't know any better
I'd love to explore further my spiritual awakening connection
The energy released is addictive

Reborn into life

Energy from somewhere
I feel so different
Releasing your inner demons
Has had a cathartic affect
Everything is lighter
No worries or stress
Was I like this before
I don't know if anyone knows
Don't keep everything in side
It will eat and rot you away
Rejuvenated is how I feel
Reborn into life once more
A tingling sensation
I forgot to mention
As you pour your heart out
Not afraid to say what's attacking you from inside out
Time is standing still I know it keeps go ticking
by, it's like nothing I've felt before
I just want to sit a while and enjoy the peace and tranquility
Is this what I've been waiting for
I know what to expect as at some stage it will trickle
away, I may not notice it will be sometime away
I appear distracted which is complete trash
My eyes are bright as a flash
No artifical stimulants
My inner laughter trickling thorough
A little girly giggle
I've never felt more in the moment
More in the present
It's strange I've got to do my job

I'm not afraid
It's like I've taken some alcoholic cool aid
Sit up and take notice of where I've been
No one really knows until a life changing
event knocks you on your bum
I may want to sit amongst and take the ambiance in
Acknowledging what a struggle it's been
I just want to go on the b of the bang
Under starters orders as I begin the race again
This time with clarity
This time rejuvenated
You see I can draw inspiration from places I haven't seen
I feel like I've a little piece of heaven following me around
An angel cloud bright and fluffy
Reborn into life
I have the inner strength to be different
Not that sluggish old woman
Somebody somewhere just give me that
chance to prove to myself again
As I have proven that I can make it back from the
murky depths of some sinister horror movie
That's been playing in the background
Don't let your hounds go from your grasp
As it proves to be a very different task

I love you

I never thought these words would resonate across my lips
Saying I love you to yourself is quite strange
It's actually very powerful
Writing a letter to yourself
People will think I'm bonkers
It took a while to convey
What I really wanted to say
Depending on what part of the day
I find it really useful
Or I find it boring and think what a silly old cow
Writing to herself now
I love you Zoë
Don't forget the dots
And put them in the right spot
The inner me talking to the rationale part of my brain
Take a look at yourself now
Wow what a difference
We all need help
A little bit of self help goes along way
I can't wait to show it
To the right people of course
It shows I've progressed
We know we all digress
And have to be strong
I will look at it on a rainy day
Maybe I should post if to myself
Receive it another way
To see how I feel
If I can say I love you Zoë again
Do I feel foolish

Or was there something ghoulish the way I said those words
Going back in time I wouldn't have the shine to put on the gloss
I would've flossed it all over until it was a sticky old mess
Then I would have to confess
That my words were untrue
Thinking about it then would make me feel really blue
Stay at a steady pace
For you to continue in this race
Believe in me when I say I love you to myself

A ball of energy

Exposing yourself like a gust of wind
So fierce and strong
You wonder what's going on
Time travels quicker than the speed of sound
You have to wait for it to catch up when the pound is strong
A ball of energy
Really addictive for my type of personality
The margins so wide
You have time to fit it all in
A manic episode
In the middle of the day
You wake up low of energy wondering what's going on
A switch to the addictive stuff with the power on
A ball of energy
A battery on full blast will eventually burn itself out
You sit and think what it's all about
Why can't I have more
Am I being tested
It like my brain sends
Texts
Snapchat
Instagram messages
Whistle and blows until my body catches up
In the meantime my brain has gone into reverse
It's in a confused state
Where many can relate
If only the middle part of the day lasted longer and longer
I wouldn't sit so deep in my head
Wondering what's lays for me when I get out of bed

Remembering things I want to do
So deeply encased in my sleepy bubble
Go back to sleep you will forget it in a minute
Minutes turn to hours
Before the strike of noon
Then it's like I've got energy and behave like a loon
It's not very productive
The energy is seductive
It doesn't come in a bottle
It doesn't come in a spray
It comes to me in the middle part of the day

The narrowest of margins

I've put my trust in you
To put trust in myself
I believe in you
Do you believe in me
Do I believe in myself
So many creative superstars falling by the wayside
In the end the dark thoughts win
Ending your daily struggle from within
What tempered those thoughts
Alcohol and drugs or a bit of both
Even just having a superhero day
Doesn't stop the dark having its play
First across the hurdle
Or last to the finishing line
How do I stop those thoughts from having a derby of a day
At Ladies Day at Royal Ascot
Or The Melbourne cup
Having a bet too see whose next up
Don't forget the ones who you left behind
Trying to find a reason to be around
Trying to maintain their place above the earth
Do you believe in me
I know you've said
Do you believe in me now
With those thoughts around my head
What stops the almighty blow out
When you thought you had just figured what life is about
Who else is worried
Who else believes in me
The thoughts that I have

It takes a courageous step to do the final bow
Not being worried, gives it another powerful
stir around the mixing bowl
Maybe I've figured it out
You have a crystal clear of a day
When that's gone you wonder why no more
So you chase that dragon for that final hit
You come to a screeching halt thinking this it
Left or right they both seem similar
Let's chase the dragon's tail
I know we're going to fail
Do you believe in me to keep on going
Battling the demons of my past
Have you put your trust in me to stay
We've put all this effort in there's no reason to go
I'm not angry with you as my time has not been wasted
I'm angry and disappointed with what I've tasted
To have this bitter taste in your mouth
Does it bother you that I'm so candid
The judicial scales of life to tip the final balance
Do you believe in me not to fail by the narrowest of margins

The penny finally drops

Finally understanding what one day, one
step, to your preferred self means
What provocative words
Keep it simple
Keep to the straight and narrow
I've stepped along these paths without really knowing
A simple conversation sets these words
free tumbling from my mouth
The hairs on my neck stuck up as if to attention
I've said something with a really deep meaning
I've read these words before, looked at them
strangely not knowing what they meant
A puzzle for me to unlock
A conundrum
A key to understanding of how I want to be
It's taken a while
I stopped and listened to the silence after
Like someone knocking on my door, pounding away wanting to
come in, a dull thud leading to a hearty knock for all to hear
SOMEONE LET ME IN
Can you tell me what this means
A picture drawn
My not preferred self
Verses
My preferred self
All very simple and childlike

I didn't know how to express fully
I understand now and it makes me happy
I want to sing I want to dance
I want to juggle up and down
One step
One day
To your preferred self
Thank you

Not now in the future

What am I going to do with my life now that I'm old and grey
What purpose do I have
Sitting watching
Sitting wondering
Contemplating my future as the years go tumbling on
Time travels faster
Who knows what my next thought will be
Contemplating my naval, as my bones creak
and my back curves inwards
Watching the ground as I slowly bend towards my knees
Why am I still thinking what purpose I have in life
Why am I planning my next move
Pondering and muddling through
Waiting for my missed opportunities
I've missed the boat on that one
I was too old for that
Why would anyone believe in me
They can see the age creeping in
Lurching and leaching into every crevice
Until someone gives you a tap in your shoulder
Who is this, you look strangely familiar
A punch in the guts leaves me winded,
unable to breathe, gulping for air
Get up listen
Holding my shoulders as a support
It's my shadow that has escaped from the black
I look refreshed
I look renewed

Looking brighter, my brain is clearer
Too bright for me to work with
Go back in the shadows I can't deal with you right now
I'm happy in this place knowing what poison to take
Punches to my head, striking on the sweet
spot, making my head spin
The new me standing threatening revenge, to rip and
shred the dark that's hanging loosely from my body
It's much better here so stop your whinging
Get up and live life to the fullest
Shake it off, shake it up
Meet me when you stop feeling sorry for yourself
Time goes passing by and spring has come
No one has come to give me that gentle push, as
a reminder that life goes on regardless
Reality sinks in, it's me who has to work
to get my life back in order
I'm old and grey and my choices are limited
Photos of my past withered and crumpled
with age, the date clearly notched
Family and friends have moved on
I sit and wonder, what life would be like if I had
chosen the light, it brings tears to my eyes
Unable to move from where I left myself so many years ago
I've failed in my quest and it's too late now
Poisoned by negativity, the dark is my only companion

I didn't know you had it in you

I did not know you had it in you
I never thought you would
Two sentences to make the hairs on the back of my neck stick up
Like molten lava cruising through my veins
My temperature rising until the steam blows out my ears
We are so different
That I don't know you can see
Through your rose tinted glasses
Everyone on the same pedestal
I never thought you would
Heard throughout my life
You know I'm stronger than that
The facts speak for themselves
From the moment I arrived
I never thought you would
Try mixing it up
I thought you would
As everyone is different from these neck of the woods
I knew you had it in you
More powerful than ever
Don't put me down there
Just don't put me down
Because my words will rise against the
injustice of those spoken against me
You know I will keep on fighting
I will scrap for every last tit bit

I will go out of my way to show everyone
With a bit more entertainment laid on
You know I'm quite high functioning in a different sort of way
I've learnt that dramas never suit
That self awareness is my key
So I'm sorry if I don't bite at your words
As they will put me spinning out of control
Confusing what is real

Over exposure 100

I can't control what people see
I can't control what people think
I can't control what people read
I wish I could control this fear of exposing my inner most feelings
Is it a fear of the truth unfolding
Is it a fear I will spiral out of control
I've no idea how to fix this feeling
When I receive feedback from my book
Anxiety and sickness
Do I stick it down a rabbit hole
And forget all about it
I'm at the Mad Hatters tea party
Sitting in a setting that's not alien to me
My eyes darting back and forth, taking in the chaos before me
My heart pumping out my chest
Breathing like I've had a packet of cigarettes
All because I've exposed myself
Not in the inappropriate way, otherwise I'd
be down the station quick smart
I'm the painting of the Scream by Munch
My shoulders go in a hunch
I stand there with my hands either side of my face
Tell me why
I feel a rush of anxiety and I want to cry
My mouth is so dry

I feel like I've been in a drought
I'd love other people's opinions
How to relieve the anxiety when others
read my inner most thoughts
I can't concentrate
I can't think
Deleting everything would be foolish
It would be a knee jerk reaction of stupidity
Of a fear I should be able to control

Yeah or nah kind of day

It really bugs me
When I don't have the motivation
Days off are gold
And your interest folds
When you go yeah nah
I will do that another day
A day turns into weeks
You look out from your covers
And go yeah nah again
Go back to sleep
Let's go play hide and seek
Which one of us will turn up today
You make excuses
It's too late in the day
Or it's too far away
I'm not miserable
I'm not depressed
I just don't have a lot of interest
It's all rather boring
I will see you in the morning
When which part of me says yes
Let's do this and let's do that
I'd love to see a change in my thinking
I'd rather be drinking
Let's hit the booze
See if you lose yourself in that haze of unforgiveness
It's not ok to do that
I'd feel like crap

A hangover would last a while
Why not go out in style
Yeah nah to that as well
Days off are gold
I've already been told
Get out and do
It ain't doing you any good
Your brain on auto pilot
Let's find the crew for this manual dysfunction
All you find is your no good for anything,
trying to live up to expectations
Wanting to have that connection that looks so powerful
The loving face, the confident smile and with a
sense of belonging in that one picture
You feel it creeping in
Like the fog rolling in
It can be so consequential
To lose your potential
On a yeah or nah kind of day

Sweet and sour pork

No wonder I'm a mess
With all this stuff to confess
To get it down on paper
I can't do it later
I never knew I had so much in my head
Laying there thinking my brain was dead
Or I was forgetful
You enlighten yourself
When you have stuff to portray
Get it off your chest
You got to do what's best
Is it a sign of loneliness
To get the stuff out your brain
Before you start the next phase of your life
It's come to fruition
With my new edition
It's holding me back
Getting my thoughts on track
Whilst preparing for work
While I'm eating my Chinese takeaway
Sweet and sour pork
Just get on my fork
Be careful of indigestion
It will teach you a lesson
To hurry your food
You're bent over double
Now you're in trouble
When you have the eye on your prize
It will be your demise
To concentrate on one thing and not the other

A gift

You lay yourself bare
By talking to her there
A gift every six weeks
I feel more refreshed
When I have given my best
My time is coming
To stop myself from returning
Why give it up
When you know you feel safe
And you set yourself free
Freeing the stuff from your head
Laying it to bed the black stuff that's been choking your soul
I haven't got much left
That makes me bereft
Sitting there twiddling a ring
I can think of the next thing
My light was infected
It's all interconnected to follow that link
That was all out of sync
I've got so much to tell
We would need a timeout bell
Verbal diarrhoea from my side at least
She's probably thinking leave me in peace
Money well spent
For no particular event
To lighten my heart and my head
To close those X Files
From those negative trials
I want to believe, that the truth is out there

To feel lighter in side
It causes a divide
From what I was then
To what I am now
To stop it returning
I have to keep working
With a great big dollop from myself
My six weeks is returning
I can't stop myself from churning
Waiting to spend a gift on me

Kindness month

Your act of kindness
Has blinded me
From the madness
That going on round here
We've all different personalities
That enable us to work in different specialties
To provide one common goal
We're here for a reason
It was no act of treason
That your kindness
Landed you in this place
Your act of kindness
Has resolved someone's darkest hour
We work four on
Two off
Until we're too old to do
Or you give me the flu
We all work together
In all kinds of weather
To support each other on the days we have to hit the floor running
Your act of kindness shows in many ways
From giving PRN
To that kind touch of a smile
We are never too busy to leave without a kind word
You make my day when you acknowledge
how busy it has been today

Green eyed monster

I'm the green eyed monster
Who wants more out of life
I see other people looking so happy and relaxed
I'm jealous and I want it really bad
It makes me tearful
It just makes me sad realising
I don't know where I'm going
I know where I've been
I'm not wasting time
I'm searching for that answer
I'm searing for that pot of gold
I can see people look so happy and connected
It makes me feel disconnected
I've got to hold on to my heart
It melts every time
We will develop relationships
We will develop bonds
Unable to break the spaghetti strings the connection is so deep
It makes me weep
Being the green eyed monster
Brings out great crushing emotions
That leave you stranded
I'm going down the only road I know
It's lonely
And I want more and more
I can taste the love
I can taste that soft loving touch
I want it so very much
I'm not satisfied with what I have

Zoë Hickerson

I'm craving more
It makes me poor
And I'm a sad old bore
Somebody scoop me up
From this life fuck up
There has to be more
Just guide me
I will go blindly if I gave you my hands
My eyes full of tears
Just stop this pain of wanting
Making me realise what I have lost along the lonely highway
Wanting perfection
I will wait a life time to come back to this spot, where the
earth opened up showing me what can be achieved
I want to believe
I don't want to deceive
I'm the green eyed monster
Please break me free from this torturous life
Of wanting

Communication

My communication isn't as it should be
I'm biting at the small stuff
I'm not communicating at all well
Sarcasm is my enemy
I don't know why it's happening
It happened last week
I'm more self aware
It's making me paranoid
If I notice
What do other people think
Eventually it will go to the top
I will be called in and my anxiety is going to pop
I've tried my CBT stuff
I'm not really sure if it's working
I don't really want to be this kind of person
It feels I'm being torn in two
Maybe it was too early to think I had settled
I'm trying to work on my communication
It's harder than you think
I begin to think I'm a failure
That's easier to think than a humongous success
Please stop the thoughts going straight to my jugular
It's spinning out of control
I worked on mindfulness before I came
in unsure of the benefit of that
My mood fluctuates from week to week
I really need a cry maybe lose control for a little bit
Climbing out of the fire again it's harder to grasp on to the truth
My truth is out there
I'm just finding it hard to find

Gutter snake

I'm sneaking around in the gutter
It's a warm and familiar place
Everyone's burning slag runs through here at a tremendous pace
Picking off people's trails and tribulations
Is a good foundation for me to build
I'm sneaking around in the gutter as I'm too lazy to rise up
I've paddled my head above water and smelt what's beyond
Too much work to keep me afloat in this virtual stinking pond
I can't hold my breath I have to keep bobbing down below
The clear air makes my lungs hurt this is what I want to show
The slurry down below gives me confidence
with all my worldly needs
Someone keeps trying to drag me along and up onto their knees
I don't want to look at them square in their face
I'm not in a hurry to win this particular race
It's a fragment of my imagination that I was always on the cusp
I'm sneaking around in the gutter looking to see what's up
Meeting Stephen King's character IT, sends a shiver down my spine
He has always been a hero of mine, so I
think we will get along just fine
Time has no ending for a misfit like me
I am comfortable being down
Flushing me through the gutter through to the other side of town
Somewhere towards the long trickle of
garbage that is floated out to sea
Am I going to be recycled and placed in someone's inventory
Stinking in someone's garbage bin rotting from down below
I can't wait to be thrown out again
As I know my journey is a constant circular connection

To the never ending flow of decomposed materials
Now I can be set free again and spread my
disease to some unexpected soul
I'm sneaking around in the gutter trying to spread
my negativity. That's my expected goal

I could be wrong

Admitting to myself that if it happened again,
I would have to choose to end my life.
The likelihood of it happening, well there's always a percentage
To avoid the feelings and stress it causes
Licking my open wounds
Rubbing the salt in
I thought the scab had formed and we were moving forward
I was wrong
Like a rocket landing in your stomach
Like an old man with breathing difficulties
Like a fountain springing a leak
Why have such a stress reaction
Asking safety questions is my job
Giving a different perspective when trying to get
my point across, just circling my issue
When they don't understand
"You's don't know me"
I was wrong
I know we only see you when you're unwell
I'm just doing my job
It's no laughing matter
Although the world should laugh with you
The questions
The paper work
The guilt
The sadness
The internal turmoil of being an incompetent human being
Would be all too much
Life is so cut and dry

It's one way or the other
Where was the in between that we know
I was wrong
I'm sorry I've been a failure
I don't really want to go
I need to work it through in my head extra hard
Use the tools
Use your tools
Use your tools that work
I guess it's in my DNA like an X or Y chromosome
I could be wrong there too

Local land fill

When the ink runs dry
All I have to do is cry
Anxiety and confusion
A foregone conclusion
I've built this brick wall
To break my fall
It makes no sense
That my thoughts are so intense
To stop that pressure cooker in my head
Steaming full of rubbish
My nightmares playing on repeat
The heat from the bottom causing steam to rise to the top
I have to be careful
My communication is a vital
So much space to fill in
After my narrow minded past
Please give me guidance
For I am at a silence
Wondering which path it will take me
I've not to be complacent about my mentality
CBT
Mindfulness etc
All that stuff works
To give you a perk
It's better than caffeine
To drink near the ravine
It makes people wince
To see yourself so pinched
I don't want to sink in that land fill over there
So much green gas, people leave you alone

Saying nothing because they don't want you to be offended
I fill up ended
As I'm paranoid about life
It's the smallest of things that stop the ink from drying
Until it spirals out of control
The baggage on your back
Is making me hack
Too late to off load in the middle of the road

Zoë Hickerson

Squatter's rights

The darkness declared squatting rights well
before I knew anything about it
Deep and insidious it went
Entrenched in my head
A battle had begun
A Mexican standoff
Until the good guys started to win
They would battle for months
Until there was bright light at the end of the tunnel
The light would win, until the dark had regrouped
and had enough cynical power to take over again
Again the light fought back with more force
The stalemate would go on for a while
Until the light was firmly fixed
Then a lot of wandering and wondering
Why do I have so much time and space
Maybe I should be doing projects
Or go out do something with my time
Reaching into the light
You find friendship, proper communication, stuff
you had enjoyed before, help and new tools.
You sit and ponder
You think wow all this time I was preoccupied
with all of this heavy stuff in my head
Where has it gone,
I've turned things around I know
Otherwise, I would never grown to know
myself how much the dark ruled
And my life nearly ended

Ticking time bomb

I'm just a ticking time bomb ready to
blow everything to smithereens
I've run over the first signs of spring
A lonely daffodil drifting in the wind
Innocently growing all alone minding its own business
Until I came along
I feel angry
I feel guilty
I feel remorse
Too many emotions in one day
I'm just a time bomb ticking its time away
I've got a bombardment going around in my head
It's been left behind since I've made progress
Now it's making me feel hopeless
Making me second guess everything I do
I don't know where my killing fields are
I don't have to travel very far
Are they on the out or are they on the in
Where ever it is, it's making my patience very thin
I need an expert sniper
To take me out
Between my eyes or just behind my ear
Two very similar sweet spots that have the same effect
Let me have that one last cigarette
I want the burn of nicotine in the back of my throat
Perhaps my second go around would be more fulfilling
My buildings are collapsing from the war inside my head
That time bomb may go off instead
Here we go down that lonely road again

Zoë Hickerson

I want to know why I'm feeling like this
Is it just another process
That lonely little daffodil swaying in the wind
It's been bent out of proportion by my heavy handedness
It's not what I'm worried about
The time bombing tick tick ticking
Is taking its time to fuse
Confusing and uncomfortable feelings around in my head
Maybe I've been given a second chance, to see if I
can work out my communication threads
The bomb disposal unit is ready and on high alert
The lonely yellow daffodil swaying happily in the spring
Stands out as the most beautiful of things

Walking the plank

In the not too distant past keys weighed me down heavily
My keys have been virtual
These keys had been locking away my
potential, I was being held prisoner
By the black inside my head
Many times I thought I was dead
The suffocation
The desolation
The wandering up and down
Not knowing which way was what
Footsteps so loud they caused ringing in my ears
I didn't know I had been like this for years
An event so powerful
Honestly I must have had a guts full
That it came spilling over the edge
Trickle by trickle my life left me
Drop by drop I was changing
I didn't know this and ignored the signs
I didn't know I was changing for the worse
It was an emotional curse
That held me tightly in its vice like grip
I was on a trip to self destruction
The keys kept on jangling silently on the outside,
inside a great cacophony of noise
Adding on another layer of poison
I needed an angel
A guiding light
A voice of reason
To stop the treason going on in my head

Zoë Hickerson

I did not have the strength to mutiny
Instead I was prepared to walk the plank
Feet first or head first to end the scrutiny
It didn't really matter
I didn't know any better
Fast forward at a slow pace
I am not in this place
Doors have been opening
The keys silently withdrawing
To give myself something to believe in
I had to face up to my demons
I have found a safe place to voice my reasons
An angel
A guiding light
A shining star
Pen, paper and iPhone notes
You have to throw away the key to get back on track
Otherwise that monkey on your back will have the last laugh
You need to hold life precariously in your grasp

Weapons of self destruction

You know yourself when taking a dive into the murky grey stuff
You don't want to admit it
Glossing it over for the loved ones who will tell you in the end
As you will beat yourself up once more
Getting in between the war in your head
We are our own worst enemy
The chat
The chastising
What thought came into my head this time
If I had my brain dissected, frozen and carved
thinly like a lovely piece of ham
What would the cross section look like
Thinly carved sections of me shooting arrows across my head
Some hitting the bullseye and bouncing off
And some straying hitting a nerve
Around the outside will be different shades of the dark
Further in towards the bullseye the dark is all encompassing
The bullseye has one word flashing red suicide
No arrows have hit this today because I
feel stronger than yesterday
Around the outside is a train, making frequent stops
to pick the weapons of mass self destruction
Sometimes empty, as I have been able to deflect
these arrows and used my tools
At times a cloud comes and blocks my view
I still shoot because I know their ultimate direction
Every section has a different war against the black and the white

Filling my head with all sort of rubbish
I want to scream and shout to get it all out
When days are calm
Peace and a ceasefire reigns
Calm blue water lapping at the side with
happiness drawn in the sand

What do I have to offer

What do I have to offer
What can I give in return
I don't know the answer to that question
Did I forget to mention
What abilities do you see
Or do you see someone without capability
What do I have to offer
When I'm full of my inner turmoil
What do I give in return
When you see an old and frail person
I don't have much to offer
As I can't see what you see
What do you see that I can offer
Someone must feel sorry to even bother
Someone must have believed
Do they believe in me now
I'm sorry I can't see what I have to offer
It must be embarrassing hiring me
Am I a liability
Isn't it blatantly obvious
I don't have much to offer
Apart from my history
Burned at the judges table
Burned out by my own guilty confessions
My session will almost be over
So I apologise if I can't see what I have to offer

Why pretend to be somebody else

Why pretend to be somebody else
Aren't you happy in your own skin
Life throws too many expectations
To know where you stand
And what you stand for
Life can be confusing
A pill for that a pill this
Throw as many obstacles
Or change the order of play
Life will always greet you the same
A beautiful sunrise in the morning
Or thunderstorm at dusk
The in between
Well that's yours for the making
Nobody said it followed a pattern
Masquerading as someone else
They will find out eventually
You can't disguise their inner equilibrium
The saying I can't catch a break, I've given up trying
The trying makes us stronger
The trying does not make us weak
Don't get lost in a sentimentalism
You will lose out when it's time
Life has so many expectations
Life has so many resources
Why pretend to be someone else

Emotionally disconnected

I'm not getting that emotional connection
I'm not getting that something
I'm realising
I must be deeply unhappy
I try not to torture myself
Into believing that I am
I'm like a squid with suckers for arms that won't let go
Black billowing out when we are in distress
I won't drain your blood
You can get on with your life without me
I'm just that sad person you see struggling and barely holding on
Hoping that life will change
I won't suck your life force
I will give it a dam good try
I know how and when I should go about it
It's so very hard to break that connection
It's mine to control, to press that magic button
I may need a slight push
Then I will feel rejected
And retreat deeper inside
Talking to myself how stupid can I be
I'm not getting that emotional connection
I must be deeply unhappy
That's why I'm here all the time
I'm like a bad smell
That comes and goes with the wind
Never really leaving
Just on the periphery
Always having one eye on the escape

The other on the prize
It's not that unusual
You see this all the time
A startled look
The adrenalin rush
I'm not the private investigator who waits on the street
corner, his hat hiding his eyes ready for the killing blow
Wanting the cash, so he can dash, so he can make the headlines
I want to enjoy that emotional connection
That desperately needs to thrive
What does the future hold before me
In this sad and unhappy life

A window through to your soul

A window through to your soul
Take a peak
Look into my eyes what do you see beyond
The tough outer coating of my hardened shell
What does it tell you
Can you see any secrets
Can you see the pain and the hurt
That have wrinkled around my eyes
Each one telling a story
Some hilariously funny
Some tragically furrowed deep into my soul
They are the keepers of dark secrets
Guarding precariously the windows of my being
Who knows what will come next
We have to be prepared
Sleep deprivation a sign of your week resolve
Tears flow freely to wash away the guilt and responsibility of
behaviours past, they flow through the craggy cracks upon
our face, moistening the foot bridge that is our castle
That is our safe haven our very own soul
Build up your reserves of tears who knows
what words will break your resilience
Our eyes look upon these words with different meaning
We reach out to others, look into their eyes seeing
the emotion beyond and the history before
Tragic sparkly blue that wind you in
You sit and look as they silently tell their story

Our windows to our souls connecting and understanding
the difference between light and dark
Some are able to stare right into your heart reach
in and twist until your blood runs thin
Encapsulating your wisdom and your essence
Until there is no life beyond just a tiny flicker
of hope that one day will spark into life

Free will

I know I'm not feeling it
I know my performance is lacking
I'm stacking up all these misdemeanours
Before anyone pulls me in
I'm angry at being angry
I know I'm not feeling it
Do I feel a guilty confessional coming along?
I know I've got to be strong
I'm disillusioned
And I can't be bothered
Surely I'm bothered
As I wouldn't be caring
I'm sharing
My self around
Just dunk me in any old bin
I'm sure I'd fit in
With poverty of thought
And my melancholic mind
I have the ability to chatrasophise
My performance is lacking
And I know I'm not feeling it
I know I'm not disappointed
Surely I'm disappointed
As I wouldn't be writing this thing
I'm really disjointed
I've gone over my virtual line

My own free will if you like
I'm sure to lay supine
To carry on without a care is a coward's way out
I've got to get to the pin point where it all went wrong
Maybe it hasn't and I'm going to sing this lonely song
I will take a look at it philosophically
I know I'm self-determined enough not to do anything idiotically

I pray for the day

I pray for the day for my pain go away
A simple wish
I put on your dish
It will be worth it
I know of no other way to break these stumbling blocks
I've been given a great deal of stick
To look back with kindness
I now have the self-awareness
It comes with light-headedness
With all the pills
Maybe they don't work and I'm the one that ills
I pray for the day to make my pain go away
It's only a simple wish
It's a 3 way thing
Maybe much more than that
Waiting for our world to collide to syncopate
Don't rush take your time
I'm looking for the signs
Rome wasn't built in a day
I grind my teeth together
I don't know what hurts its altogether
Wanting to cry
Or swear out loud
It's all on high alert
The desperation you feel whether mental or physical
Good and evil are inextricably linked
In a metaphysical battle across the space and time continuum
Pray for me on this day

I'm not offended

I'm not offended
By your slovenly ways
It's what I expect
Sitting and waiting for an important call
It's the way we defend our integrity
A fortunate stroke of serendipity
Has got us thus far
We raise the bar
So we can venture wide
I want to know who is on your side
Wherever we ride
On the open road
I'm offended
By the way I have become
Slow as a sloth
Give me a cloth
To wipe the negativity of my mind
I'm sure the pain killers have been unkind
Mangling my ability to think
Clearly there is a difference
For me that's a major hindrance
Why do I feel so alive?
When I feel dead inside
I'm not offended to feel like that
It's par for the course
When my body wants a divorce
Let's get the ball rolling
I see no need for stalling
Who knows how painful it can be

Make use of your silence

The quietness for a depressive
Is never aggressive
It stumbles in quiet as a mouse
When it gets dark all over the house
A membrane thick and throbbing around my peripheral vision
Slowly slowly
Until there is a tiny pin prick of light
Try seeing the world through that
Try seeking the truth
The truth has been leeched out
There is no colour
There is nothing that I can do
A silence
What I thought was a quiet day
Has backfired beyond my imagination
I don't know
I don't want
I wish for a swish of a magic wand
A pumpkin made from a stagnant pond
Will transform my night
Where I will dance without disinhibition
A folklore born out of tradition
To find my maiden banished into a corner
Come follow my hand
Because this is where you should stand

Zoë Hickerson

My imaginary life
Turns back to black
As I sit with this silence
Pills scattered indiscriminately
How many do I have left?
Don't bother to count
Don't bother to care
As I will be soon out of your hair
Make use of your silence
Where ever you sit
You can retrieve someone from their cold desolate pit

Second skin

Second skin
Is only as thin as you like
The second born look all forlorn
Always one step behind the first
Teachers and the like
Go on strike
When the second child enters the room
The first has set the president
The second just a bad smell
You could do better if he or she was here as well
The seconds are always different
The seconds are fiercely independent
The first try get to get all the adulation
Yes we are treated differently
You have to be a second to figure it out
Tried and tested on the first
Old and worn on the second
New blue prints
The seconds wants to sprint
To dust off the claustrophobic misrepresentation
We all understand
We're all in that collective
We know we're never guaranteed to be the leader of the pack

CPSIA information can be obtained
at www.ICGtesting.com
Printed in the USA
BVHW041645090321
602013BV00007B/1442